She Plays Sports

# She Plays Soccer

By Trudy Becker

I0877445

level 2 little blue readers

www.littlebluehousebooks.com

Copyright © 2023 by Little Blue House, Mendota Heights, MN 55120. All rights reserved. No part of this book may be reproduced or utilized in any form or by any means without written permission from the publisher.

Little Blue House is distributed by North Star Editions:
sales@northstareditions.com | 888-417-0195

Produced for Little Blue House by Red Line Editorial.

Photographs ©: iStockphoto, cover, 4, 7, 11, 12, 16, 19, 21, 23, 24 (top left), 24 (top right), 24 (bottom left), 24 (bottom right); Shutterstock Images, 9 (top), 9 (bottom), 15

**Library of Congress Control Number: 2022910478**

**ISBN**
978-1-64619-710-1 (hardcover)
978-1-64619-742-2 (paperback)
978-1-64619-802-3 (ebook pdf)
978-1-64619-774-3 (hosted ebook)

Printed in the United States of America
Mankato, MN
012023

## About the Author

Trudy Becker lives in Minneapolis, Minnesota. She likes exploring new places and loves anything involving books.

# Table of Contents

# Getting Ready

I play soccer.

I love game days.

I get ready to play.

I put on my uniform.

I wear shorts and a jersey.

I match my team.

jersey

I put on my shin guards and socks.
They keep my legs safe.
I put on my cleats.
They help me run fast.

shin guard

cleats

I fill my water bottle and pick up my soccer ball. I put everything in my bag.

soccer ball
water bottle

goal

# On the Field

Games happen on the soccer field.

The field has white lines on it.

There is a big goal at each end.

Fans watch from the side of the field.
They cheer for the players.

fans

# In the Game

I listen for the whistle.

It blows to start each game.

I keep my hands away.

They can't touch the ball.

I dribble the ball down the field.

I kick the ball with my right foot.

Then I use my left foot.

dribble

Sometimes I can't take a shot.

So, I look around the field.

I pass the ball.

10
4

Other times, I shoot the ball toward the goal.

I kick it hard.

I score!

I love soccer.

# Glossary

**dribble**

**jersey**

**goal**

**soccer ball**

# Index